"The victory will be determined by the first blow of your sword."
- Yagyu Munenori

Copyright © Michael Jacyna

All rights reserved. No part of this publication may be reproduced or used in any way or means, electronic or mechanical, including photocopying and recording without prior written permission from the author.

For further information on this and other aikido related books visit:
ExploreAikido.com

ISBN-13: 978-1948038027

Library of Congress Control Number: 2017916461

Explore AIKIDO Vol. 3

Aiki-Ken *Sword Techniques in Aikido*

Michael Jacyna

Content

Preface 7

Aiki-ken etiquette 8

Aiki-ken forms & technical aspects 14

Aiki-ken suburi 20

Aiki-ken fundamental kihons 44

Aiki-ken yokomen kihons 98

Aiki-ken advanced kihons 123

Ken nage 144

Ken dori 170

Kumi tachi 199

Glossary 211

Preface

Aiki-ken is an inseparable part of aikido training. It is one of the three main areas of aikido study. Aiki-tai jutsu, aiki-jo, and aiki-ken compose aikido as one cohesive art form.

In this volume, I strive to present aiki-ken sword techniques from an accessible and transparent viewpoint. Keep in mind, however, that as transparent and visually accessible this volume may be, it is not a substitute for training in a dojo under the guidance of a qualified and knowledgeable teacher who can present, explain, and clarify the nuances of each technique.

For those who have yet to experience aikido, I hope this book will inspire and ignite your journey. For aikido enthusiasts, I hope this book will serve as a fundamental guide. As for seasoned aikidokas, I hope this book will provide you with thought provoking material.

I would like to express my gratitude and appreciation to my instructors who have influenced me both on and off the mat: Jacek Wysocki, and the late Giampietro Savegnago, thank you.

I would like to thank my students: Aaron Bush, Marie Visisombat, Zachary Nikolayev and Andrey Yevdoshchenko, for their time, effort, and dedication during the photo-shoots, and the making of this book.

Aiki-Ken Etiquette

Aiki-ken training, same as aiki-tai jutsu and aiki-jo, begins and ends with etiquette. Incorporating etiquette within aiki-ken practice creates mutual respect among all participants in the class and results in organized and safe training environment.

There are a few things to remember during aiki-ken etiquette. At a lineup in seiza, the bokken shall be placed on the left side at a slight angle, so that the handle points toward one's center line, with the bokken's blade directed outward. When standing, the bokken should be held in the left hand, at hip level, blade facing up. The entire handle should be exposed, and the end of the handle should be on one's center line at all times. Even when bowing, the bokken should stay in the same position, without moving up and down.

On the following pages you can see a few examples of bowing and transferring of the bokken between teacher and students and peer-to-peer.

Bow between teacher and student

Usually, when a teacher and student bow to each other during aiki-ken training, the teacher bows while standing and the student bows in seiza. This is also implemented when a student assists the instructor during presentation and/or after receiving advice during practice (pic. 1-4).

Bokken transfer between teacher and student

When transferring the bokken between teacher and student, the teacher is standing, while the student is seated. In the example below, the instructor transfers the bokken to the student. At that time, the teacher holds the bokken with the blade directed toward himself. As the bokken changes hands, the student flips the bokken, so that the blade is directed toward the student. Simultaneously both the teacher and student bow. Once the bokken is received, the student places the bokken on the left side, blade directed outward (pic. 1-8).

Bow between peers

When students bow to each other in seiza, the bokken is placed at an angle on their left side. The handle should be closer to their center line, and the blade directed outward (pic. 1-5).

Tachi rei, Standing bow between peers with the bokken

When students bow to each other, they hold their bokkens, so that the entire handle is exposed, with the blade facing up. During tachi rei, the bokken should stay in place without moving down or up. Only student's upper body should go into the bow (pic. 1-5).

Bokken transfer between peers

When transferring the bokken between peers, one student presents the bokken with the blade directed toward herself. As the bokken changes hands, the student receiving the bokken turns the blade toward himself, bowing simultaneously; then places the bokken to his left side (pic. 1-6).

Aiki-Ken Forms & Technical Aspects

In aiki-ken training, same as in aiki-jo, there is a standard weapon size. The standard bokken length is between 39.25-41 inches or 100-104cm. There are exceptions to this rule. The width and shape may vary slightly, based on the style of the bokken. For example, suburito ken tends to be longer and heavier, and is meant for suburi only, as a supplemental training tool. Note that in kids' training, the bokken sizing may need to be adjusted. Quality bokken is made by hand from Japanese white oak. This gives the weapon great durability, excellent weight distribution, and balance.

Aiki-ken Forms. There are five different arrangements in which aiki-ken can be practiced:

1. Bokken suburi is a repetitive practice of singular strikes, blocks, entries, and other basic moves.

2. Bokken kihon are forms that consist of suburi. They can be practiced alone or with a partner.

3. Ken nage is part of aiki-ken where we use the bokken to throw uke.

4. Ken dori are disarming techniques against uke attacking with the bokken.

5. Kumi tachi is a set up where both shite (defender) and seme (attacker) are equipped with the ken.

Aiki-ken Technical Aspects. There are a few things to remember during aiki-ken training. They will help organize and understand the system.

1. Holding the bokken

When we work with and hold the bokken with both hands, the left grip is on the bottom and the right grip is located above the left grip. Depending on the maneuver or action performed, the span between left and right hand grip may vary. In techniques where we hold the bokken with one hand, we take into account the potential grip placement of the other hand. For example, at the beginning of kihons we start with the right hand grip only. The grip is already in place where it belongs, approximately in the middle of the handle, leaving room for the placement of the left hand grip. See few bokken grip examples below:

At the beginning of kihon, right hand grip only, in the middle of the handle (pic. 1).

At the final kaeshi position, two hands grip, the left on the bottom, the right hand above (pic. 2).

At the final one hand full extension tsuki position, left hand grip at the end of the handle (pic. 3).

2. No guard at the beginning of techniques

In aiki-ken, same as in aiki-tai jutsu and aiki-jo, there is no guard at the beginning of techniques. View the example of a ken dori technique. Uke begins with shomen uchi attack, and tori is in a right profile stance without a guard, basically waiting until it is too late for uke to change or adjust the direction of the attack. Then, tori moves forward, enters, and executes the desired technique (pic. 1-3).

3. Distance

Distance is an important element within aiki-ken. Please see examples of different aiki-ken training set ups below and the appropriate distance.

In **kumi tachi**, ken against ken, training distance is approximately one tatami length, which is equal to roughly six and a half feet or two meters. In other words, it is a distance where to reach their partner, the other person would need to take one step forward (pic. 1).

Ken nage, training where we use the bokken to throw the uke. Distance in this case is also one step away. Meaning, uke is one step away from reaching tori (pic. 2).

Ken dori, disarming techniques against the bokken attack. Same as before, the distance is one step away. Meaning, the attacker is one step away from reaching the defender (pic. 3).

4. Bokken extends from the center line

The bokken should extend from the hara, or from one's own center line. For example, at the end of a tsuki thrust, if we drew a line from the handle back, the line should end up coming toward our center line and the obi or hakama knot (pic. 1).

5. Profile position

During aiki-ken, we should be in a profile position, meaning, always on one or the other side of the bokken. We should never be in a square position, unless a particular technique or maneuver calls for it. View example of tsuki in left profile stance (pic. 1).

6. Center line control

Center line control in aiki-ken is a very important element and also a recurring concept throughout all aikido areas, including aiki-tai jutsu and aiki-jo.

7. Oto nashi no ken - silent bokken

This is an innovative and efficient concept. Basically, it comes down to the ability of executing techniques, without your opponent's touching or being able to block your ken. Incorporating this element, developing of understanding, finesse and ability to put it into practice make aiki-ken quick, smooth and efficient, but also require a lot of training.

8. Bokken striking parts

Bokken is a wooden weapon and has no real sharp blade. We do, however, handle the bokken as if it had one. In most cases, we use the bokken as a striking weapon rather than a cutting weapon. Most strikes are applied with kensaki, the tip of the bokken's blade, and mono uchi, 4-8 inches of the blade closest to the kensaki. There are exceptions to that rule. An example would be using tsuka, the handle of the bokken, to apply atemi.

9. Shochikubai - three friends of winter symbolize pine, bamboo, plum

Aiki-ken kihons can be categorized into the following larger groups. Ume no tachi are kihons that begin from the ground up (*ume* is plum in Japanese and symbolizes rebirth and growth). Take no tachi are kihons that incorporate mainly uke nagashi (*take* is bamboo in Japanese and symbolizes strength and flexibility). Matsu no tachi are kihons that begin from the top (*matsu* is pine in Japanese and symbolizes longevity, virtue, and youth).

10. Bokken striking target areas

There are a few basic striking areas in aiki-ken. View some of the examples below:

1. Forehead/head

2. Temple/neck

3. Abdomen

4. Throat/face

5. Wrist(s)

6. Groin

11. Parts of the bokken

1) Kensaki - tip of the bokken's blade. 2) Mono uchi - 4-8 inches of the blade closest to the kensaki.
3) Ha - edge of the blade. 4) Mune - back of the blade. 5) Shinogi - blade ridge.
6) Tsuba - hand guard. 7) Tsuka - handle. 8) Kashira - tsuka's back end.

Aiki-Ken Suburi

Suburi training, a repetitive practice of singular strikes, blocks, entries, and other basic moves. It is a good way to develop proper technique, posture, speed, strength, resistance, and body coordination.

Aiki-ken suburi · shomen uchi - square shoulder width stance; front view

Shomen uchi is one of the basic strikes and usually the first one new students are exposed to and learn. Begin in shoulder width square stance and the bokken at judan no kamae (pic. 1). Raise your bokken all the way up, onto your back, and then return with shomen uchi (pic. 2-6).

Aiki-ken suburi · shomen uchi - square shoulder width stance; profile view

Profile view of the same exercise as shown on the previous page.

Aiki-ken suburi · shomen uchi - shiko dachi stance; front view

Begin in shiko dachi stance and the bokken at judan no kamae (pic. 1). Raise the bokken all the way up and onto your back, then execute shomen uchi (pic. 2-6).

Aiki-ken suburi · shomen uchi - shiko dachi stance; profile view
Profile view of the same exercise as shown on the previous page.

Aiki-ken suburi · shomen uchi - square shoulder width stance - with squatting; front view

Begin in shoulder width square stance and the bokken at judan no kamae. Then strike one shomen uchi in standing position and the next one while squatting (pic. 1-6).

Aiki-ken suburi · shomen uchi - migi hanmi stance - with squatting; front view

Begin in right profile stance and the bokken at judan no kamae. Then strike one shomen uchi in standing position and the next one while squatting (pic. 1-6).

Aiki-ken suburi · shomen uchi - hidari hanmi stance - with squatting; front view

Begin in left profile stance and the bokken at judan no kamae. Then strike one shomen uchi in standing position, and the next one while squatting (pic. 1-6).

Aiki-ken suburi · shomen uchi - migi hanmi stance forward & back jumps; profile view.

Begin in right profile stance and the bokken at judan no kamae. Raise the bokken, start shomen uchi, and simultaneously jump forward. As you jump back, raise the bokken (pic. 1-6).

Aiki-ken suburi · yokomen uchi - shiko dachi stance; front view

Begin in shiko dachi stance and the bokken at judan no kamae (pic. 1). Raise the bokken all the way up, then execute jodan yokomen uchi (pic. 2-4). Raise the bokken back up and execute jodan yokomen uchi on the other side (pic. 5-8). Note that the initial movement for yokomen uchi is the same as that for shomen uchi. This suburi can be performed in a variety of ways. For example, you can add different levels for the target, such as jodan/jodan, judan/judan, gedan/gedan, and so on.

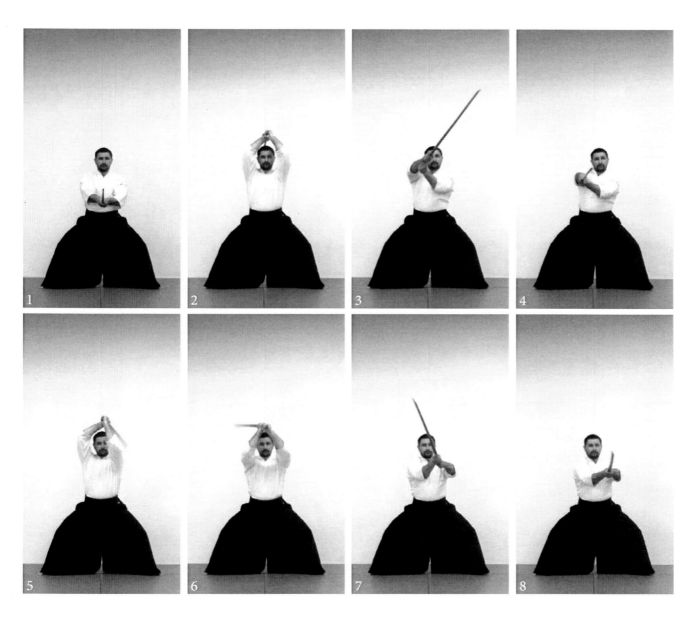

Aiki-ken suburi · yokomen uchi - migi hanmi, top to bottom/bottom to top; front view

Begin in right profile stance and the bokken at judan no kamae. Then start with right side yokomen uchi and cut all the way down (pic. 1-4). Immediately return on the same path with ume no tachi (pic. 5-7). Execute left side yokomen uchi and immediately return in the same trajectory with ume no tachi (pic. 8-12).

Aiki-ken suburi · yokomen uchi - hidari hanmi, top to bottom/bottom to top; front view

Begin in left profile stance and the bokken at judan no kamae, then start with left side yokomen uchi and cut all the way down (pic. 1-4). Immediately return on the same path with ume no tachi, then execute right side yokomen uchi (pic. 5-10). Return in the same trajectory with ume no tachi (pic. 11-12).

Aiki-ken suburi · shomen uchi - migi hanmi, static strike on the line; front view

Begin in right profile stance and the bokken on the center line at judan no kamae (pic. 1). Raise the bokken all the way up, onto your back, then return with shomen uchi (pic. 2-4). During this suburi, which is in a profile position, make sure to maintain a straight trajectory of the bokken on the center line.

Aiki-ken suburi · shomen uchi - migi hanmi, dynamic attack on the line; front view

Begin in right profile stance and the bokken on the center line at judan no kamae (pic. 1). Raise the bokken all the way up, onto your back, and then return with shomen uchi (pic. 2-6). This suburi is a shomen uchi attack during which we move forward. During shomen uchi, it is important to release the bokken first, then follow with your body.

Aiki-ken suburi · shomen uchi - migi hanmi, dynamic counter attack off the line; front view

Begin in right profile stance and the bokken on the center line at judan no kamae (pic. 1). Raise the bokken all the way up, onto your back, then return with shomen uchi (pic. 2-6). This suburi is a shomen uchi counter attack, during which we move forward and off the line. During this suburi, make sure to initially move forward and at the last moment move your back hip off the line. At the end, you should be off the line and only the kensaki should stay on the line.

Aiki-ken suburi · shomen uchi - hidari hanmi, static strike on the line; front view

Begin in left profile stance and the bokken on the center line at judan no kamae (pic. 1). Raise the bokken all the way up, onto your back, then return with a shomen uchi strike (pic. 2-5). During this suburi, which is in a profile position, make sure to maintain straight trajectory of the bokken on the center line.

Aiki-ken suburi · shomen uchi - hidari hanmi, dynamic attack on the line; front view

Begin in left profile stance and the bokken on the center line at judan no kamae (pic. 1). Raise the bokken all the way up, onto your back, then return with shomen uchi (pic. 2-6). This suburi is a shomen uchi attack during which we move forward. During shomen uchi, it is important to release the bokken first, then follow with your body.

Aiki-ken suburi · shomen uchi - hidari hanmi, dynamic counter attack off the line; front view.

Begin in left profile stance and the bokken on the center line at judan no kamae (pic. 1). Raise the bokken all the way up, onto your back, then return with shomen uchi (pic. 2-6). This suburi is a shomen uchi counter attack, during which we move forward and off the line. During this suburi, make sure to initially move forward, then, at the last moment, move your back hip off the line. At the end, you should be off the line, and only the kensaki should stay on the line.

Aiki-ken suburi · tsuki - migi hanmi, dynamic attack on the line; profile view

Begin in right profile stance and the bokken on the center line at judan no kamae (pic. 1). Move slightly forward and bring the bokken handle toward your center (pic. 1-2). Move forward and release tsuki (pic. 3-6).

Explore Aikido Vol. 3

Aiki-ken suburi · tsuki - migi hanmi dynamic attack; front view
Front view of the same attack as shown on the previous page.

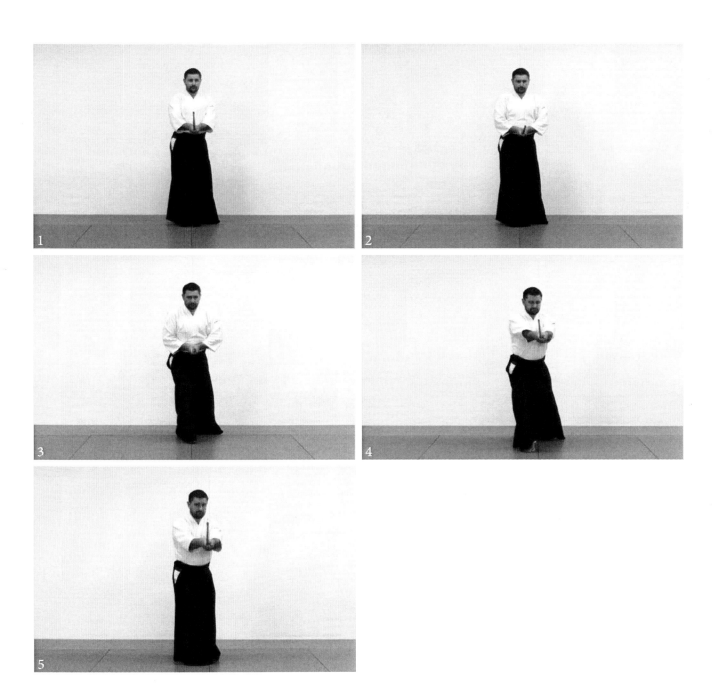

Uke nagashi is an absorbing/deflecting maneuver, usually followed by an immediate or slightly delayed strike or thrust. There are a few basic uke nagashi options in aiki-ken.

Aiki-ken suburi · ue no uke nagashi - migi hanmi; profile, front and rear view

The first uke nagashi is Ue, which means up or above. Begin in right profile stance, with the bokken in jodan no kamae (pic. 1). Bring your hands above and in front of your forehead, so that the bokken is pointing forward with the blade facing up (pic. 2). From this position, continue and execute kaeshi (pic. 3).

Pictures 1-3 show ue no uke nagashi, front view.
Pictures 4-6 show ue no uke nagashi, rear view.

Aiki-ken suburi · shita no uke nagashi - migi hanmi; profile view

The second uke nagashi is Shita, which means down or below. Begin in right profile stance, with the bokken in judan no kamae (pic. 1). Lower the kensaki to gedan level (pic. 2). Resurface back to judan or jodan level and step forward (pic. 3-5).

Aiki-Ken Fundamental Kihons

Aiki-ken fundamental kihons · kihon #1

Begin in right profile stance and execute shomen uchi off the line (pic. 1-3). Continue with tsuki judan (pic. 4-5). Follow up with shita no uke nagashi and finish with tsuki jodan (pic. 6-8).

This kihon falls into the larger *take no tachi* group.

Aiki-ken fundamental kihons · kihon #2

Begin in right profile stance and execute tsuki judan off the line (pic. 1-4). Continue with shomen uchi (pic. 5-7). Follow up with ue no uke nagashi and finish with kaeshi (pic. 8-12).

This kihon falls into the larger *take no tachi* group.

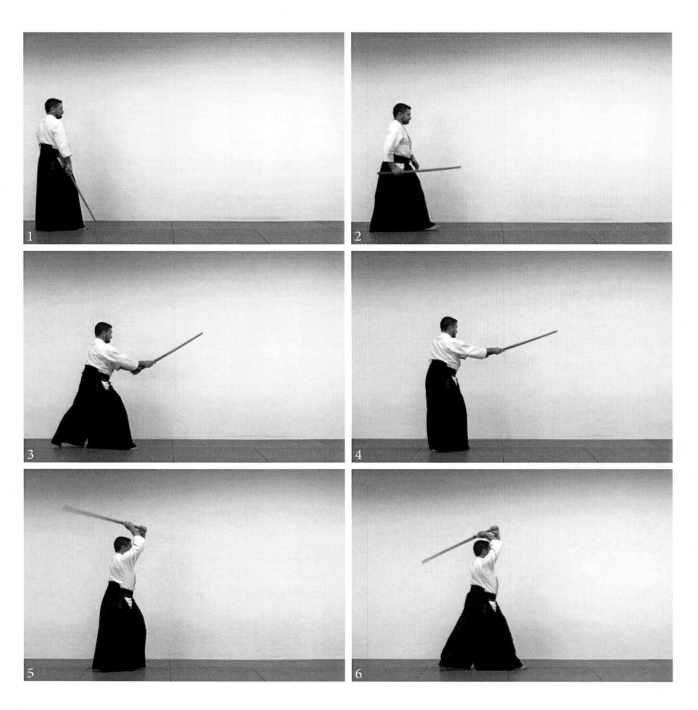

Aiki-ken fundamental kihons · kihon #3

Begin in right profile stance and execute shomen uchi off the line (pic. 1-5). Continue with ue no uke nagashi (pic. 6-7) and finish with kaeshi (pic. 8-10).

This kihon falls into the larger *take no tachi* group.

Aiki-ken fundamental kihons · kihon #4

Begin in right profile stance and execute tsuki judan off the line (pic. 1-3). Continue with shita no uke nagashi (pic. 4-5) and finish with tsuki jodan (pic. 6-8).

This kihon falls into the larger *take no tachi* group.

Aiki-ken fundamental kihons · kihon #5

Begin in right profile stance and execute furi komi tsuki slightly off the line (pic. 1-4). Continue with ue no uke nagashi and finish with kaeshi (pic. 5-10).

This is the first kihon from the fundamental kihons group that falls into the larger *ume no tachi* group.

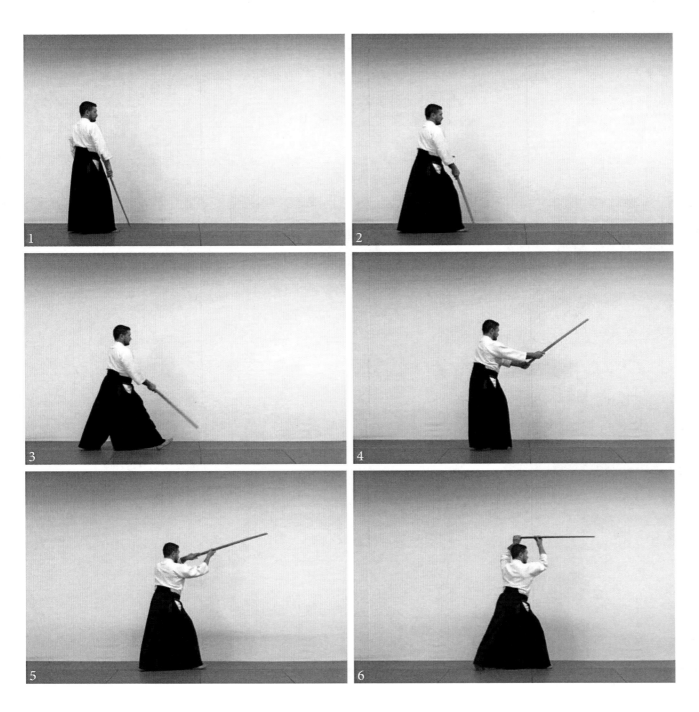

Aiki-ken fundamental kihons · kihon #6

Begin in right profile stance and execute tsuki jodan off the line (pic. 1-5). Continue with ue no uke nagashi and finish with kaeshi (pic. 6-10).

This kihon falls into the larger *take no tachi* group.

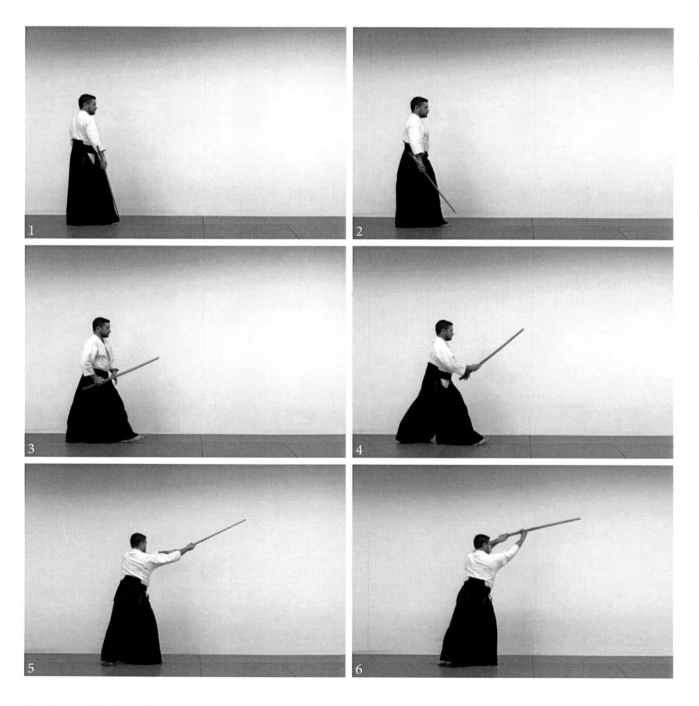

Aiki-ken fundamental kihons · kihon #7

Begin in right profile stance and execute shomen uchi, with irimi off the line (pic. 1-5). Continue with shita no uke nagashi and finish with tsuki jodan (pic. 6-9).

This kihon falls into the larger *take no tachi* group.

Aiki-ken fundamental kihons · kihon #8

Begin in right profile stance and execute shomen uchi off the line (pic. 1-4). Continue with ue no uke nagashi and kaeshi (pic. 5-7). Follow up with another ue no uke nagashi and finish with kaeshi (pic. 8-10).

This kihon falls into the larger *take no tachi* group.

Aiki-ken fundamental kihons · transitional kihon between #8 & #9

Begin in right profile stance and execute shomen uchi off the line (pic. 1-4). Continue with ue no uke nagashi and kaeshi (pic. 5-7). Follow up with shita no uke nagashi and finish with tsuki jodan (pic. 8-10).

This kihon falls into the larger *take no tachi* group.

Aiki-ken fundamental kihons · kihon #9

Begin in right profile stance and execute tsuki judan off the line (pic. 1-3). Continue with shita no uke nagashi and tsuki judan (pic. 4-6). Follow up with another shita no uke nagashi and finish with tsuki (pic. 8-9).

This kihon falls into the larger *take no tachi* group.

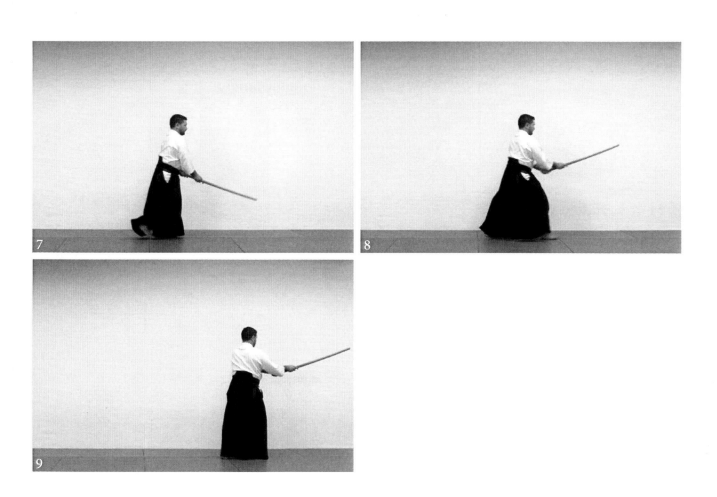

Aiki-ken fundamental kihons · kihon #10

Begin in right profile stance and execute ume no tachi off the line (pic. 1-5). Immediately continue with men uchi (pic. 6-7). Follow up with ue no uke nagashi and finish with kaeshi (pic. 8-11).

This kihon falls into the larger *ume no tachi* group.

Aiki-ken fundamental kihons · kihon #11

Begin in left profile stance, step forward, and execute furi komi tsuki (pic. 1-4). Retract into hasso no kamae (pic. 5-6). Continue with ume no tachi and open your center line to lure in your opponent's attack (pic. 7-9). Finish with men uchi off the line (pic. 10-12).

This kihon falls into the larger *ume no tachi* group.

Aiki-ken fundamental kihons · kihon #12

Begin in right profile stance and raise the bokken as if attacking with shomen uchi (pic. 1-3). Start to rotate off the line and around your vertical center line (pic. 4-5). Finish off the line with matsu no tachi cut from the top (pic. 6-9).

This is the first kihon from the fundamental kihons group that falls into the larger *matsu no tachi* group.

Aiki-ken fundamental kihons · kihon #13

Begin in right profile stance and raise the bokken as if attacking with shomen uchi (pic. 1-3). Start to rotate slightly off the line and around your vertical center line (pic. 4-5). Finish off the line with men uchi and zanshin (pic. 6-9).

This kihon falls into the larger *matsu no tachi* group.

Aiki-ken fundamental kihons · kihon #14

Begin in right profile stance, move slightly forward, and execute tsuki with the kashira (the back end of the handle) (pic. 1-3). Continue and finish with ume no tachi (pic. 4-9).

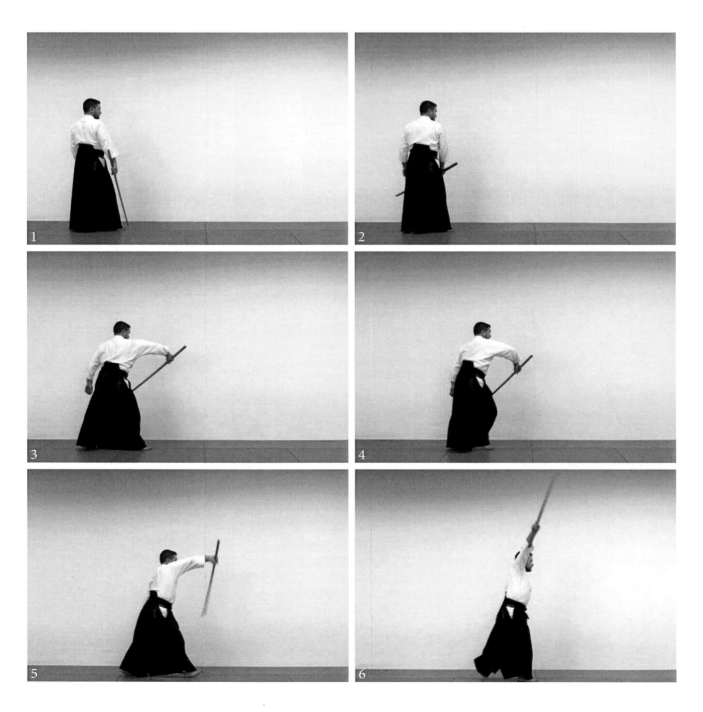

Aiki-ken fundamental kihons · kihon #15

Begin in right profile stance, move slightly back, and simultaneously bring the bokken behind your back (pic. 1-4). Finish with men uchi off the line (pic. 5-8).

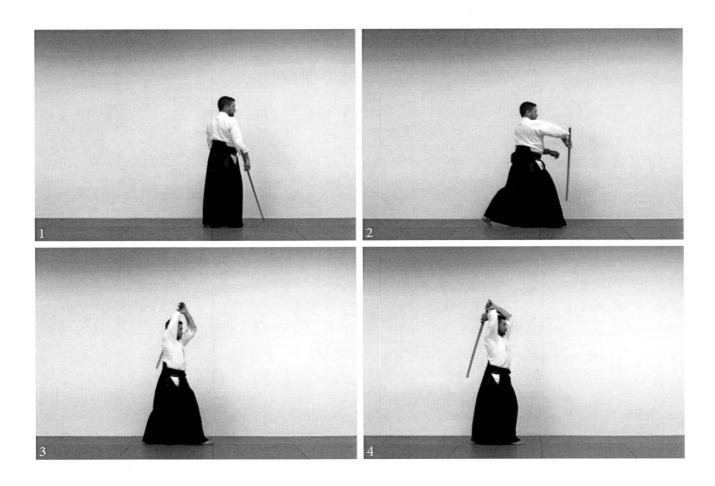

Aiki-ken fundamental kihons · kihon #16

Begin in right profile stance, move back and off the line, and execute tsuki jodan (pic. 1-7).

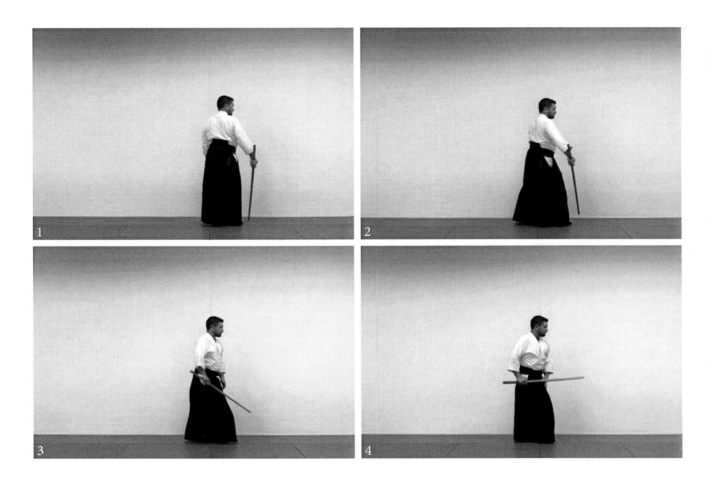

Aiki-ken fundamental kihons · kihon #17

Begin in right profile stance and execute men uchi (pic. 1-4). Step forward and finish with tsuki jodan (pic. 5-8).

Aiki-ken fundamental kihons · kihon #18

Begin in right profile stance, raise the bokken up, and simultaneously move forward (pic. 1-3). Cut horizontally from right to left using uke nagashi, then move off the line to the left (pic. 4-8).

Aiki-ken fundamental kihons · kihon #19

Begin in right profile stance, raise the bokken up, and simultaneously move forward (pic. 1-4). Cut horizontally from left to right using uke nagashi, then move off the line to the right (pic. 5-8).

Aiki-ken fundamental kihons · kihon #20

Begin in right profile stance, step back, and execute ume no tachi (pic. 1-7).

Aiki-ken fundamental kihons · kihon #21

Begin in right profile stance, step back and off the line, then execute tsuki jodan (pic. 1-8).

Aiki-ken fundamental kihons · kihon #22

Begin in left profile hasso no kamae, step back, and execute furi komi tsuki (pic. 1-6). Finish in right profile hasso no kamae (pic. 7-8).

Aiki-ken fundamental kihons · kihon #23

Begin in left profile hasso no kamae, step back and off the line, and execute tsuki jodan (pic. 1-8).

Aiki-ken fundamental kihons · kihon #24

Begin in right profile stance, step back, and execute ume no tachi (pic. 1-4). Step back again and finish tsuki jodan (pic. 5-9).

Aiki-ken fundamental kihons · kihon #25

Begin in right profile stance and execute shomen uchi (pic. 1-6). Immediately continue with ume no tachi and finish off the line to the right (pic. 7-10).

This kihon is also called *tsubame kaeshi* which, in Japanese, means "turning swallow cut". Both the downward and upward cuts should be performed in one quick continuous motion.

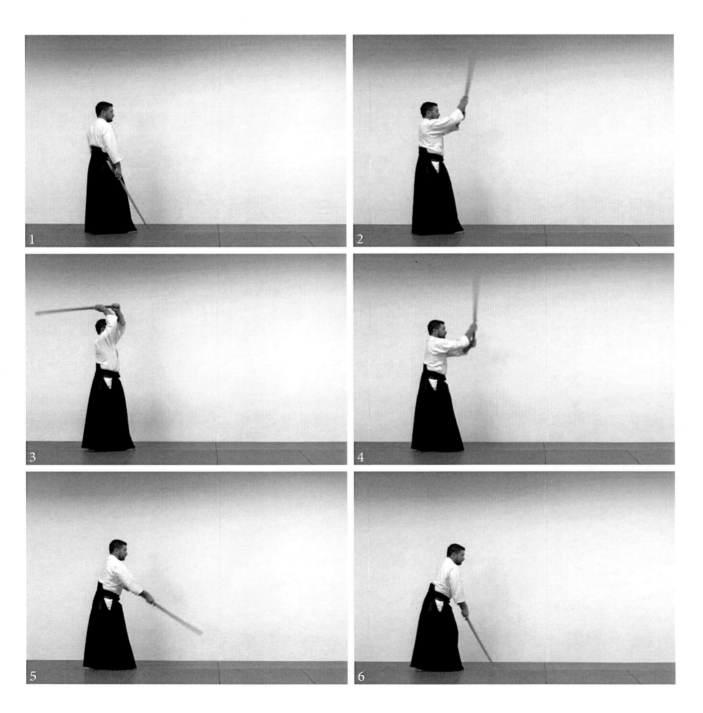

Aiki-ken fundamental kihons · kihon #26

Begin in right profile stance and execute a swift horizontal cut at eye-level on a crescent trajectory (pic. 1-9).

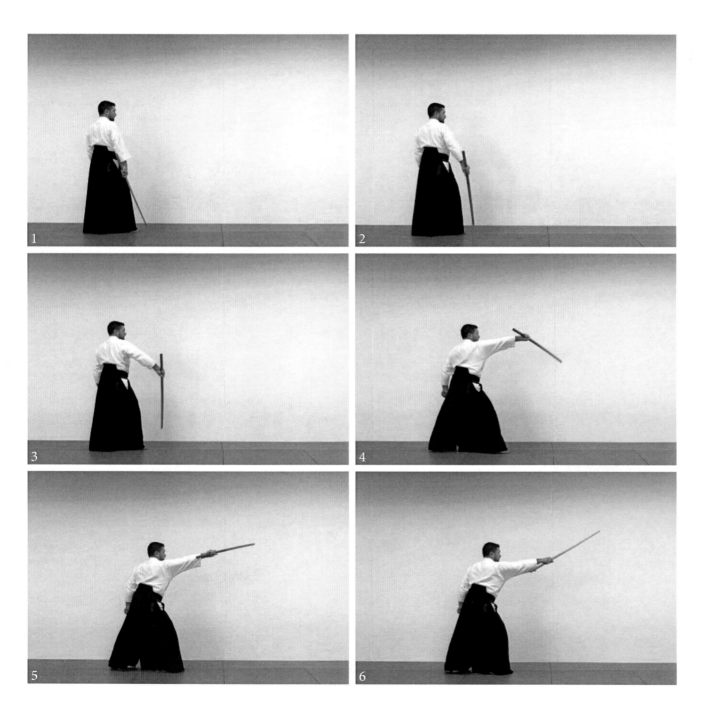

Aiki-Ken Yokomen Kihons

Aiki-ken yokomen kihons · kihon #1

Begin in left profile stance and raise the bokken (pic.1-3). Execute shomen uchi irimi without deviating off the line (pic. 4-8).

Aiki-ken yokomen kihons · kihon #2

Begin in left profile stance, raise the bokken, and execute shomen uchi (pic. 1-6). Continue with ue no uke nagashi and finish with kaeshi (pic. 7-11).

Aiki-ken yokomen kihons · kihon #3

Begin in left profile stance, raise the bokken, and execute shomen uchi (pic. 1-5). Continue with shita no uke nagashi and finish with tsuki jodan (pic. 6-10).

Aiki-ken yokomen kihons · kihon #4

Begin in left profile stance, raise the bokken, and execute yokomen uchi all the way through. Simultaneously step forward and off the line (pic. 1-8).

Aiki-ken yokomen kihons · kihon #5

Begin in left profile stance, raise the bokken, and execute yokomen uchi (pic. 1-5). Immediately move forward with tsuki jodan (pic. 6-8).

Aiki-ken yokomen kihons · kihon #6

Begin in left profile stance, raise the bokken, and execute yokomen uchi (pic. 1-5). Retract the bokken slightly and, with a short delay, move forward with tsuki jodan (pic. 6-8).

Aiki-ken yokomen kihons · kihon #7

Begin in left profile stance, raise the bokken, and execute yokomen uchi (pic. 1-4). Retract the bokken, move back, and slightly turn away (pic. 5-6). Return and finish with tsuki jodan (pic. 7-8).

Aiki-ken yokomen kihons · kihon #8

Begin in left profile stance, raise the bokken, and execute yokomen uchi (pic. 1-4). Retract the bokken, simultaneously step forward, and execute tsuki jodan (pic. 5-7).

Aiki-ken yokomen kihons · kihon #9

Begin in left profile stance, raise the bokken, and execute yokomen uchi (pic. 1-5). Retract the bokken, then enter with the bokken diagonally at jodan level (pic. 6-8). Finish with stepping off the line and executing a cut at eye level (pic. 9).

Explore Aikido Vol. 3

Aiki-ken yokomen kihons · kihon #10

Begin in left profile stance and raise the bokken as if getting ready to strike men uchi (pic. 1-3). Move forward and execute ume no tachi (pic. 4-7). Finish in hasso no kamae off the line (pic. 8-9).

Aiki-ken yokomen kihons · kihon #11

Begin in left profile stance and raise the bokken as if getting ready to strike men uchi (pic. 1-3). Step forward, descend into half position off the line, and simultaneously execute uke nagashi (pic. 4-8).

Aiki-ken yokomen kihons · kihon #12

Begin in left profile stance and raise the bokken as if getting ready to strike men uchi (pic. 1-3). Step forward and simultaneously execute uke nagashi (pic. 4-7). Follow up with irimi tenkan and finish with men uchi (pic. 8-10).

Aiki-Ken Advanced Kihons

Aiki-ken advanced kihons · kihon #1

Begin in left profile stance, step forward, and execute tsuki jodan (pic. 1-3). Continue with ue no uke nagashi and kaeshi (pic. 4-8). Retract the bokken, move back, and slightly turn away (pic. 9). Return and finish with tsuki jodan (pic. 10-12).

Aiki-ken advanced kihons · kihon #2

Begin in left profile stance, step forward, and execute tsuki jodan (pic. 1-3). Continue with ue no uke nagashi and kaeshi (pic. 4-7). Step forward and execute ume no tachi (pic. 8-11). Finish in hasso no kamae off the line (pic. 12).

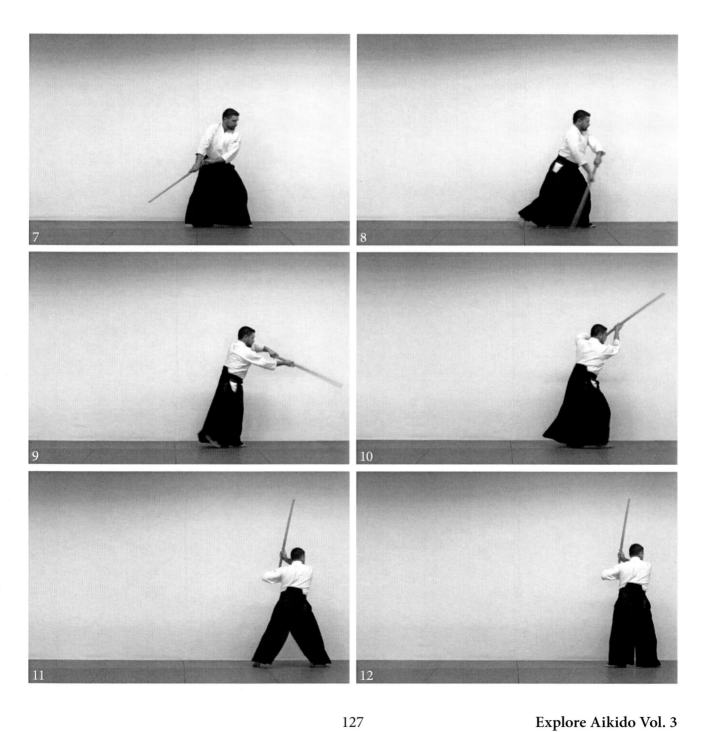

Aiki-ken advanced kihons · kihon #3

Begin in left profile stance, step forward, and execute tsuki jodan (pic. 1-3). Continue with ue no uke nagashi and kaeshi (pic. 4-6). Step back and execute ume no tachi (pic. 7-9). Without delay step back again and finish with one more ume no tachi (pic. 10-14).

Aiki-ken advanced kihons · kihon #4

Begin in left profile stance, step forward, and execute tsuki jodan (pic. 1-3). Continue with ue no uke nagashi and kaeshi (pic. 4-7). Bring the bokken back, move back, and slightly turn away (pic. 8-9). Move forward and execute soft cut at eye level (pic. 10-12). Step through and finish off the line (pic. 13-14).

Explore Aikido Vol. 3

Aiki-ken advanced kihons · kihon #5

Begin in left profile stance, step forward, and execute tsuki jodan (pic. 1-3). Continue with ue no uke nagashi and kaeshi (pic. 4-6). Bring the bokken back and continue with men uchi attack (pic. 7-9). Retract the bokken, then enter with your bokken diagonally at jodan level. Finish with stepping off the line and executing a cut at eye level (pic. 10-12).

Explore Aikido Vol. 3

Aiki-ken advanced kihons · kihon #6

Begin in right profile stance and execute shomen uchi off the line (pic. 1-4). Continue with ue no uke nagashi and kaeshi, then bring the bokken to gedan level (pic. 5-8). Step back off the line and finish with tsuki jodan (pic. 9-10).

Aiki-ken advanced kihons · kihon #7

Begin in right profile stance and execute shomen uchi with irimi off the line (pic. 1-4). Continue with shita no uke nagashi and tsuki jodan (pic. 5-7). Follow up with shita no uke nagashi, then raise the bokken all the way up (pic. 8-10). Start to rotate slightly off the line, around your vertical center line, and finish off the line with matsu no tachi cut from the top (pic. 12-14).

Aiki-ken advanced kihons · kihon #8

Begin in right profile stance, execute tsuki judan on the line and then open your center line (pic. 1-5). Continue with furi komi tsuki, ue no uke nagashi, and kaeshi (pic. 6-9). Bring the bokken to gedan level and finish with ume no tachi (pic. 10-14).

Aiki-ken advanced kihons · kihon #9

Begin in left profile stance, raise the bokken, and execute yokomen uchi (pic. 1-4). Retract the bokken and enter with furi komi tsuki (pic. 5-7). Continue with uke nagashi and finish with kiri otoshi (pic. 8-12).

Aiki-ken advanced kihons · kihon #10

Begin in right profile stance, move forward, and execute shomen uchi (pic. 1-3). Continue with tsuki judan, then uke nagashi, and kaeshi (pic. 4-10). Bring the bokken to gedan level (pic. 11). Follow up with uke nagashi and finish with horizontal jodan strike (pic. 12-16).

143 Explore Aikido Vol. 3

Ken Nage

Ken nage · attack presentation

The concept of ken nage techniques is based on uke preventing tori from pulling out and using the bokken. You can see an example below when a standard attack is applied during ken nage training. To prevent tori from pulling out the bokken, uke approaches and takes control of tori's right wrist. At the same time, uke strikes tsuki jodan with the left hand (pic. 1-4).

Ken nage · control presentation

Control in ken nage techniques is exercised by not allowing uke approach within reaching distance and by quickly drawing the bokken onto uke's center line at jodan level (pic. 1-4).

Ken nage · ikkyo omote

Begin in right profile stance (pic. 1). As uke approaches, pull the bokken slightly out and let uke catch your right wrist (pic. 2-3). Absorb uke in and execute ikkyo omote, during which time the bokken's blade is over uke's head (pic. 4-8). Zanshin is optional within most ken nage techniques (pic. 9-10).

Explore Aikido Vol. 3

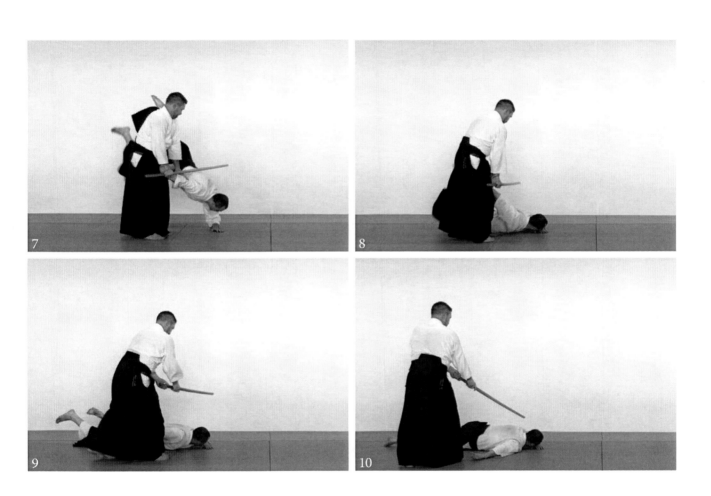

Ken nage · nikyo

Begin in right profile stance (pic. 1). As uke approaches, pull the bokken slightly out and as you lift your right forearm, let uke catch your right wrist (pic. 2-3). With the right hand and the tsuka, continue on a spiral trajectory toward uke's center and execute nikyo (pic. 4-7). Finish with zanshin (pic. 8-9).

Ken nage · sankyo

Begin in right profile stance. As uke approaches, pull the bokken slightly out. At the moment of uke's connection, step back and place your left hand onto uke's elbow (pic. 1-2). Pivot and bring uke with you by applying pressure on uke's elbow (pic. 3-4). As uke comes around, slide your left hand from elbow onto uke's wrist and take over sankyo hold. Hold and apply tsuki with kashira. Then pull the bokken out and move under uke's arm (pic. 5-7). Turn toward uke and while holding sankyo with the left hand, apply ume no tachi toward uke's face (pic. 8-9). Execute sankyo with the bokken's blade behind uke's neck (pic. 10-11). Finish with zanshin (pic. 12).

Explore Aikido Vol. 3

Ken nage · yonkyo

Begin in right profile stance (pic. 1). As uke approaches, pull the bokken slightly out. As you lift your right forearm, let uke catch your right wrist (pic. 2-3). Place the tsuka on top of uke's right forearm and pull it down and toward yourself (pic. 4-5). Finish with zanshin (pic. 6-8).

153

Explore Aikido Vol. 3

Ken nage · kotegaeshi

Begin in right profile stance (pic. 1). As uke approaches, pull the bokken slightly out and let uke catch your right wrist (pic. 2-3). Absorb uke in and wrap the tsuka around uke's right forearm from the inside out (pic. 4-5). Execute kotegaeshi and finish with zanshin (pic. 6-9).

Explore Aikido Vol. 3

Ken nage · tenchi nage

Begin in right profile stance (pic. 1). As uke approaches, pull the bokken slightly out. At the moment of uke's connection, step back and place your left hand onto uke's elbow (pic. 2-3). Pivot and bring uke with you by applying pressure on uke's elbow (pic. 3-4). As uke comes around, take control of uke's right wrist and simultaneously pull out the bokken (pic. 5). Execute tenchi nage by bringing uke forward and entering with the bokken onto uke's center line (pic. 6-9). Finish with zanshin (pic. 10).

Explore Aikido Vol. 3

Explore Aikido Vol. 3

Ken nage · ude kime osae

Begin in right profile stance (pic. 1). As uke approaches, pull the bokken slightly out. At the moment of connection, step back and place your left hand onto uke's elbow (pic. 2-3). With a vertical elliptical motion, press onto uke's elbow and execute ude kime osae (pic. 4-6). Finish with zanshin (pic. 7-9).

Explore Aikido Vol. 3

Ken nage · ude kime nage

Begin in right profile stance (pic. 1). As uke approaches, pull the bokken slightly out. At the moment of connection, place your left hand onto uke's elbow and step back (pic. 2-4). By applying pressure on uke's elbow and simultaneously stepping forward, execute ude kime nage (pic. 5-6). Finish with zanshin (pic. 7-9).

Explore Aikido Vol. 3

Ken nage · yoko irimi

Begin in right profile stance (pic. 1). As uke approaches, pull the bokken slightly out and begin stepping back. As uke connects, continue pulling forward with your right hand. Use your left arm to enter onto uke's center line and execute yoko irimi (pic. 2-6). Finish with zanshin (pic. 7-8).

Ken nage · yoko irimi #2

Begin in right profile stance (pic. 1). As uke approaches, pull the bokken slightly out and begin stepping back. As uke connects, continue pulling forward with your right hand, and use your left arm to enter onto uke's center line (pic. 2-4). Wrap your left arm around uke's neck and simultaneously pull out the bokken (pic. 5-7). Release uke from the hold and finish with zanshin (pic. 8-10).

Ken nage · koshi nage

Begin in right profile stance. As uke approaches, slightly pull out the bokken. At the moment of connection, step back and place your left hand onto uke's elbow (pic. 1-2). Pivot and bring uke with you by applying pressure on uke's elbow (pic. 3-4). As uke comes around, slide your left hand from elbow to uke's wrist and take over sankyo hold. Release uke's grip, load uke onto your hips, and execute koshi nage (pic. 5-9). Finish with zanshin (pic. 10-11).

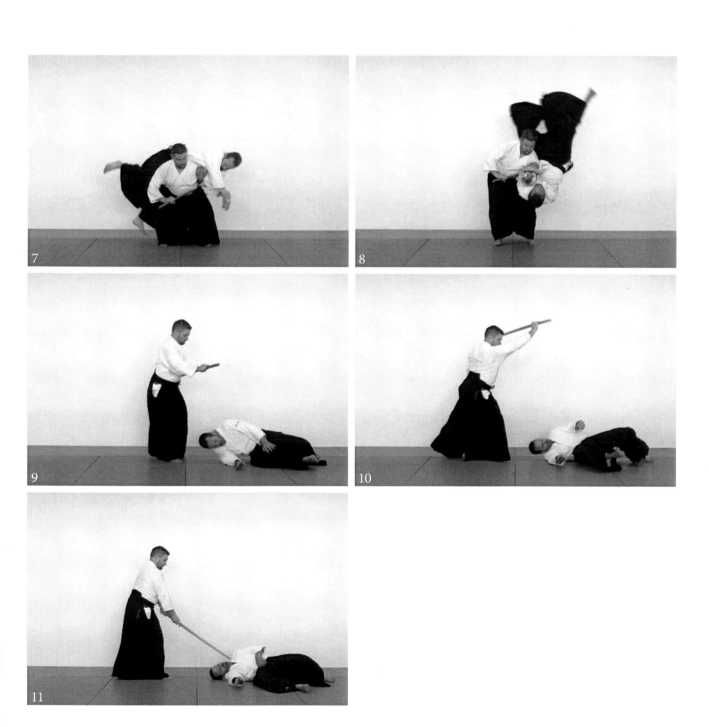

Ken nage · shiho nage irimi

Begin in right profile stance. As uke approaches, slightly pull out the bokken. At the moment of connection, step back and place your left hand onto uke's elbow pit (pic. 1-2). Bring uke forward and fold uke's left arm. As uke passes by, enter onto uke's center line with the tsuka and execute shiho nage irimi (pic. 3-7). Finish with zanshin (pic. 10-11).

Ken Dori

Ken dori · kokyu nage

Uke begins shomen uchi attack in right profile stance. As uke approaches, move forward and slightly off the line, and take over the tsuka (pic. 1-4). Continue and bring uke into kuzushi. Step forward and finish kokyu nage (pic. 5-8).

Ken dori · nikyo omote

Uke begins shomen uchi attack in right profile stance. As uke approaches, move forward and slightly off the line, briefly connect with uke's tsuka grip, and bring it down (pic. 1-4). Apply atemi with your right elbow and take over uke's right hand and the tsuka (pic. 5-6). Continue with a pivot and apply nikyo omote (pic. 7-10). Finish with zanshin (pic. 11-12).

Ken dori · sankyo omote

Uke begins shomen uchi attack in right profile stance. As uke approaches, move forward and slightly off the line. Briefly connect with uke's tsuka grip and bring it down (pic. 1-4). Apply atemi with your right elbow, take over uke's right hand and the tsuka, and continue with a pivot (pic. 5-6). From nikyo hold, take over sankyo, release the bokken from uke's grip, and apply ume no tachi toward uke's face (pic. 7-10). Execute sankyo omote with the bokken's blade behind uke's neck (pic. 11-13). Finish with zanshin (pic. 14).

Ken dori · kotegaeshi

Uke begins shomen uchi attack in right profile stance. As uke approaches, move forward and slightly off the line and use your left hand to apply atemi (pic. 1-4). Take over uke's right hand and the tsuka, bring uke sideways, and execute kotegaeshi (pic. 5-11). Finish with zanshin (pic. 12).

Ken dori · ude kime osae

Uke begins shomen uchi attack in right profile stance. As uke approaches, move forward and slightly off the line. Briefly connect with uke's tsuka grip and bring it down (pic. 1-4). Apply atemi with your right elbow and take over uke's right hand and the tsuka (pic. 5-6). Continue with a pivot and, as uke comes around, wrap your left arm around uke's right elbow, lock it, and execute ude kime osae (pic. 7-11). Finish with zanshin (pic. 12).

Ken dori · ude kime nage

Uke begins shomen uchi attack in right profile stance. As uke approaches, move forward and slightly off the line to the left. Use your right hand to take over uke's right hand and the tsuka (pic. 1-3). With your left arm, enter under and against uke's right arm and execute ude kime nage (pic. 4-7). Finish with zanshin (pic. 8-9).

Ken dori · shiho nage

Uke begins shomen uchi attack in right profile stance. As uke approaches, move forward and slightly off the line. Use your left hand to take over uke's right hand and the tsuka. Use your right hand to apply atemi (pic. 1-4). Add your right hand onto tsuka, step back with a pivot, and execute shiho nage (pic. 5-9). Finish with zanshin (pic. 10-12).

Ken dori · koshi nage #1

Uke begins shomen uchi attack in right profile stance. As uke approaches, move forward and slightly off the line to the left. Use your right hand to take over uke's right hand and the tsuka (pic. 1-3). With your left arm, enter under uke's right elbow, bring uke into kuzushi, load uke onto your hips, and execute koshi nage (pic. 4-8). Finish with zanshin (pic. 9-10).

Explore Aikido Vol. 3

Ken dori · koshi nage #2

Uke begins shomen uchi attack in right profile stance. As uke approaches, move forward and slightly off the line, then take over the tsuka (pic. 1-4). Bring uke into kuzushi, load uke onto your hips, and execute koshi nage (pic. 5-8). Finish with zanshin (pic. 9).

Explore Aikido Vol. 3

Ken dori · juji garami

Uke begins shomen uchi attack in right profile stance. As uke approaches, move forward and slightly off the line. Briefly connect with uke's bokken grip and bring it down (pic. 1-4). With your right elbow, apply atemi and take over uke's right hand and the tsuka (pic. 5). Continue with pivot, take over uke's left wrist with your left hand. Release uke's left hand grip from the bokken (pic. 6-7). Wrap uke's left arm over the right and execute juji garami (pic. 8-10). Finish with zanshin (pic. 11-12).

Explore Aikido Vol. 3

Ken dori · irimi nage

Uke begins shomen uchi attack in right profile stance. As uke approaches, move swiftly forward and slightly off the line. Immediately enter with open-palm direct irimi nage (pic. 1-8).

Ken dori · yoko irimi

Uke begins shomen uchi attack in right profile stance. As uke approaches, simultaneously step back and use your right hand to take over uke's right hand and the tsuka. Bring uke forward and execute yoko irimi by entering onto uke's center line with your left elbow (pic. 1-6). Finish with zanshin (pic. 7-9).

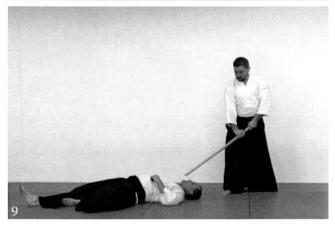

Ken dori · yoko irimi #2

Uke begins shomen uchi attack in right profile stance. As uke approaches, change your profile position. Take over uke's right hand and the tsuka and bring it down. With your left elbow, apply atemi (pic. 1-4). Stretch uke and wrap your left arm around uke's neck. Pull the ken from uke's grip and release uke from your left arm hold (pic. 5-10). Finish with zanshin (pic. 11-12).

Ken dori · ume no tachi

Uke begins shomen uchi attack in right profile stance. As uke approaches, move forward and slightly off the line. Use your right hand to take over the tsuka (pic. 1-4). Place your left palm on top of the mune, step back with a pivot, and execute ume no tachi onto uke's center line (pic. 5-9).

Kumi Tachi

Kumi tachi · fundamental kihon #1

Both shite and seme begin in right profile stance (pic. 1). Seme attacks with shomen uchi; shite counters with shomen uchi off the line (pic. 1-3). Seme moves back to avoid the counter; shite continues with tsuki judan (pic. 4-5). Seme moves back again to avoid the tsuki and attempts to block the attack. Shite responds with shita no uke nagashi and finishes with tsuki jodan and zanshin (pic. 6-9). Kihon ends when seme lets the bokken down (pic. 10).

Kumi tachi · fundamental kihon #5

Both shite and seme begin in right profile stance (pic. 1). Seme attacks with shomen uchi; shite moves forward and executes furi komi tsuki. To avoid the tsuki, seme moves back (pic. 2-5). As seme regains balance and is about to attack with shomen uchi, shite continues with ue no uke nagashi and finishes with kaeshi and zanshin (pic. 6-9). Kihon ends when seme lets the bokken down (pic. 10).

Kumi tachi · fundamental kihon #13

Both shite and seme begin in right profile stance (pic. 1). Raise the bokken as you would when attacking with shomen uchi (pic. 1-2). At the moment when you lift the bokken, seme immediately attacks with tsuki jodan. At the same time, start to rotate slightly off the line and around your vertical center line (pic. 3-4). Finish off the line with shomen uchi and zanshin (pic. 5-6). Kihon ends when seme lets the bokken down (pic. 7).

Kumi tachi · yokomen kihon #1

Shite begins in left profile stance and seme begins in right profile stance (pic. 1). Seme attacks with yokomen uchi, and shite simultaneously moves forward and executes shomen uchi irimi (pic. 2-8).

Kumi tachi · advanced kihon #2

Shite begins in left profile stance and seme begins in right profile stance (pic. 1). Seme attacks with yokomen uchi, while shite steps forward and executes tsuki jodan (pic. 2-3). Attempting to block the counter attack, seme moves back (pic. 4-5). Shite continues with ue no uke nagashi and kaeshi. To avoid the strike, seme again moves back (pic. 6-7). As shite's bokken passes, seme attacks with shomen uchi. Shite moves forward and executes ume no tachi (pic. 8-12).

Explore Aikido Vol. 3

Japanese - English Glossary

Ai - harmony
aiki-jo - aikido training with wooden staff
aiki-ken - aikido training with wooden sword
arigato - thanks, thank you
ashi - foot, leg
ashikubi - ankle
atemi - strike, blow
ayumi ashi - regular step, ordinary walking, where the legs move forward alternately

Bokken - wooden sword
budo - Japanese martial arts
bushi - warrior
bushido - feudal-military Japanese code of behavior followed by the samurai

Chikama - shortest distance, face to face with the opponent
chudan - middle position

Dan - black belt rank
deshi - student
do - way, path
dojo - martial arts studio
domo arigato gozaimashita - thank you very much (used after each class to your partner and sensei)
dori - grab, hold

Futari Dori - training against two opponents

Geri - kick
gedan - lower position
godan - 5th degree black belt rank
gyakuhanmi - opposite stance, mirrored stance

Ha - edge of bokken's blade
hachidan - 8th degree black belt rank
hai - yes
hakama - traditional Japanese pants usually worn by black-belt ranks or senior students
hara - abdomen
hanmi handachi waza - aikido practice in seated position against standing attacker(s)
hidari - left
hiji - elbow
hiza - knee

Irimi - entering movement
irimi nage - entering throw, one of the fundamental aikido techniques

Jo - wooden staff
jo dori - techniques for disarming an opponent equipped with jo
jo omote - take your jo
jo ite - place your jo away
jodan - upper position
judan - 10th degree black belt rank

Kaeshi waza - counter techniques
kai - organization
kamae - position, stance
kamiza - an alter, place of honor. In the dojo it refers to a place where the portrait(s) of the school predecessor(s) and/or calligraphy scroll is displayed
kashira - back end of bokken's handle
keiko - training
ken dori - techniques for disarming an opponent equipped with the bokken
ki - mind, spirit, energy
kihon - basic form
kensaki - tip of the bokken's blade
kokoro - heart, spirit
kokyuho - way or method of breathing
kokyu nage - "breath throw" techniques
kote - wrist
kotegaeshi - outward wrist turn or twist
kubi - neck
kuzushi - off balance position/unbalancing the opponent
kyu - any rank below black belt
kyudan - 9th degree black belt rank

Ma-ai - correct, proper distance
mae - front
meguri - flexibility and rotation of the forearms
men - face
mokuso - meditation
mono uchi - 6-8 inches of the blade closest to the sword's/bokken's tip
mune - 1) chest; 2) back of the bokken's blade
mushin - lit. no mind

Nage - throw
nanadan - 7th degree black belt rank
nanakyo - seventh pin
nidan - 2nd degree black belt rank
Nippon - Japan

O - grand, big
O'Sensei - grand master, in aikido this title refers to the founder of aikido, Morihei Ueshiba
obi - belt
omote - in the front direction (in aikido we can divide techniques into omote and ura)
onegai shimasu - in aikido training it is used at the beginning of each class and it can be understood as "please let me train with you"

Rei - bow
rokudan - 6th degree black belt rank
ryu - in budo it refers to school or style

Sandan - 3rd degree black belt rank
saya - scabbard
shiho nage - throw in four directions
seika tanden - central point of stomach located slightly below the navel
shikko - knee walking
seiza - kneeling seated position
seme - attacker, term especially used during aiki-ken and aiki-jo training. In aiki-tai jutsu the term would be replaced with "uke"
sensei - teacher, master, instructor
shite - defender, term especially used during aiki-ken and aiki-jo training. In aiki-tai jutsu the term is replaced with "tori"
shihan - master instructor
shinogi - bokken's blade ridge
shodan - 1st degree black belt rank
shomen - front or top of head
sode - sleeve
soto - outside, on the outside
suburi - basic jo or bokken practice in striking and thrusting
suwari waza - techniques in sitting position

Tachi waza - standing techniques
tai sabaki - body movements related to specific aikido techniques
tai jutsu - the art of the body (in aikido - unarmed techniques)
tachi rei - bow in standing position
tanto - knife. In aikido the term refers to wooden knife.
tatami - mat, padded flooring
te gatana - "hand sword"
tera - temple (body part)
toma - big distance
tori - the one who is carrying out the technique, the thrower. Also see "shite"
tsugi ashi - sliding and follow up step. Tsugi ashi vs. ayumi ashi
tsuba - bokken's hand guard
tsuka - bokken's handle
tsuki - punch

Uchi - open hand strike
uchi deshi - live-in student, direct student of the sensei
uke - attacker, person being thrown. Also see "seme"
ukemi waza - the art of falling in response to a technique
ura - rear
ushiro - behind, backward

Waza - technique, method, group of techniques

Yame - stop
yoko - side
yokomen - side of the head
yondan - 4th degree black belt rank
yudansha - any black belt rank holder

Zanshin - lit. remaining mind; alerted state of mind right after performing technique(s)
zarei - bow in a seiza
zori - sandals
zubon - pants

Japanese Counting

ichi - one
ni - two
san - three
shi/yon - four
go - five
roku - six
shichi/nana - seven
hachi - eight
kyu - nine
ju - ten

Other books of interest. Available from Amazon.com and other book stores.

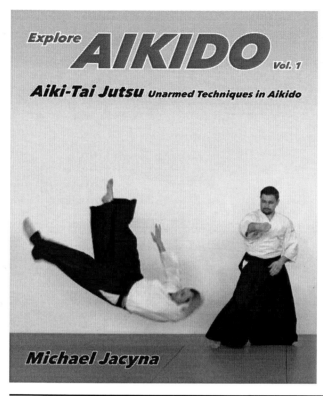

Explore AIKIDO Vol. 1
Aiki-Tai Jutsu
Unarmed Techniques in Aikido

The volume showcases wide range of unarmed aikido techniques including:

- Suwari Waza
- Hanmi Hantachi Waza
- Tachi Waza
- Futari Dori
- Randori
- Kaeshi Waza
- Ukemi Waza

ISBN-13: 978-1948038003
ISBN-10: 1948038005

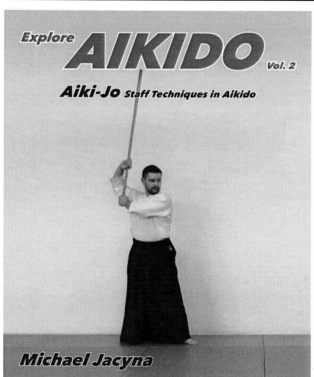

Explore AIKIDO Vol. 2
Aiki-Jo
Staff Techniques in Aikido

The volume showcases a wide range of staff techniques in aikido including:

- Aiki-Jo Etiquette
- Jo Suburi
- Jo Kihon/Kata
- Jo Nage
- Jo Dori
- Kumi Jo

ISBN 13: 978-1948038010
ISBN 10: 1948038013

Made in United States
North Haven, CT
09 August 2023